Note to Parents and Teachers

The SCIENCE STARTERS series introduces key science vocabulary to young children while encouraging them to discover and understand the world around them. The series works as a set of graded readers in three levels.

LEVEL 1: BEGINNING TO READ
These books can be read alone or as part of guided or group reading.
Each book has three sections:

• Information pages that introduce new words. These key words appear in bold throughout the book for easy recognition.
• A lively story that recalls this vocabulary and encourages children to use these words when they talk and write.
• A quiz and word search ask children to look back and recall what they have read.

MAKE IT BRIGHT looks at LIGHT AND DARK. Below are some answers and activities related to the questions on the information spreads that parents, carers, and teachers can use to discuss and develop further ideas and concepts:

p. 5 *What do you use to find your way in the dark?* Touch and hearing can help us to find our way when we can't see. Blindfold games can help children to explore these senses.

p. 7 *What time is it when the sun appears again?* It is morning/daytime. Ask children to discuss how it changes from light to dark and vice versa at sunset and sunrise.

p. 9 *What other lights does a car have?* Point out lights inside and outside a car, such as brake lights, sidelights, warning lights, dashboard lights, inside light for reading maps etc.

p. 11 *When else do people use candles?* On special occasions, e.g. on a birthday cake, at religious festivals such as Christmas and Divali, and during power failures when there is no electricity to power other lights.

p. 13 *What do red and green lights on a switch tell you?* Red and green lights are used on switches and machines such as computers, ovens, and TVs to show they are on/off.

p. 15 *What happens when the sun goes behind a cloud?* The sky gets darker. On a day when there is sunshine and some clouds, take children out to see how the light changes as the sun moves behind and emerges from a cloud. Explain that the sun is a source of light even when it is behind a cloud. Do remind children not to look directly at the sun.

p. 17 *What other lights do you see at night?* e.g. house lights, car lights.

p. 21 *Why should you wear reflective strips at night?* Shiny or reflective strips help you stand out in the dark so that drivers can easily see you if you are near a road.

ADVISORY TEAM

Educational Consultant
Andrea Bright—Science Coordinator, Trafalgar Junior School

Literacy Consultant
Jackie Holderness—former Senior Lecturer in Primary Education, Westminster Institute, Oxford Brookes University

Series Consultants
Anne Fussell—Early Years Teacher and University Tutor, Westminster Institute, Oxford Brookes University

David Fussell—C.Chem., FRSC

CONTENTS

© Aladdin Books Ltd 2007

Designed and produced by
Aladdin Books Ltd

First published in
the United States in 2007 by
Stargazer Books
c/o The Creative Company
123 South Broad Street
P.O. Box 227
Mankato, Minnesota 56002

Printed in the United States
All rights reserved

Editor: Sally Hewitt
Design: Flick, Book Design
and Graphics
Picture Research:
Alexa Brown

Thanks to:
• The pupils of Trafalgar Infants School
for appearing as models.
• Debbie Staynes for helping to organize
the photoshoots, and the pupils and
teachers of Trafalgar Junior School and
St. Nicholas C.E. Infant School for
testing the sample books.

Library of Congress Cataloging-in-Publication Data

Pipe, Jim, 1966-
   Light and dark / by Jim Pipe.
    p. cm. -- (Science starters. Level 1)
   Includes index.
   ISBN 978-1-59604-079-3
   1. Light--Juvenile literature.
   I. Title. II. Series.

QC360.P573 2006
535--dc22

           2005057638

Photocredits:
*l-left, r-right, b-bottom, t-top,
c-center, m-middle*
Front cover tl, 6br, 32tr —
Stockbyte. Front cover tm & tr,
2bl, 3, 7, 9b, 13t, 15b, 16b, 19b,
23tr, 32ml, 32br — Corbis. Front
cover b, 11br — Roger Vlitos
/ Select Pictures. 2tl, 9tr, 27br —
Comstock. 2ml, 12tr, 26 both,
27tl — Jim Pipe. 4, 17, 31mr —
Photodisc. 12b — EU. 5, 13br,
23b, 31tr, 32tl — istockphoto.com.
6t, 10, 14, 16tr, 19, 21, 24tr,
31ml, 31br, 32mlb, 32mr — US
Navy. 8tr, 20 all, 25tr, 27ml,
32mlt, 32bl —Ingram Publishing.
8b — TongRo. 11tl, 32mrt —
Flick Smith. 15tl, 22tl, 24bl, 28-29
all, 30 — Marc Arundale / Select
Pictures. 18, 22b, 32br —
Corel. 25b — Select Pictures.

SCIENCE STARTERS

LEVEL

LIGHT AND DARK

Make It Bright

by Jim Pipe

Stargazer Books

We **see** with our eyes.

When there is **light**,
we can **see** things around us.

We **see** shapes and colors.

When there is no **light**,
we cannot **see** anything. It is **dark**.

If we turn on a **light**,
we can **see** again.

• What do you use to find your way in the dark?

The **sun** lights our world.

When the **sun** is in the sky, it is **day**.

After the
sun sets,
it is **night**.

6

At **night,** it is dark outside.
We need other lights to see.

• What time is it when the sun appears again?

The **bulb** in a **lamp** makes light.
A **lamp** lights up a whole room.

Can you see the
lamps in this picture?

Bulb

8

A **flashlight** has a **bulb**.
It lights up a small area.

A car's headlights
light up the road.

• What other lights does a car have?

A **fire** gives off light, too.
Yellow **flames** look best in the dark.

Watch out! **Flames** can burn you.
Always let adults light **fires**.

Candles light
up a dark room.

The **candle** in this lantern
makes it look spooky!

• When else do people use candles?

Lights in different **colors**
show us what to do.

A red traffic light
says, "Stop!"
A green light says, "Go."

Lights show an airplane where to land.

12

Ambulance

Flashing lights **warn** cars, "Watch out!"

A **flashing** lighthouse **warns** ships, "Keep away from the rocks!"

Lighthouse

• What do red and green lights on a switch tell you?

13

Lamps and candles give off light.
They are called **light sources**.

Some **light sources** are very **bright**.
Floodlights light up a football field.

14

The sun is a very bright **light source**.
We say it **shines**.

Never look
at the sun.
It can burn
your eyes.

• What happens when the sun goes behind a cloud?

What lights up the night?

The **moon** shines in the night sky.
Stars twinkle.

Street lights
light up
the streets.

In a storm, **lightning** lights
up the night.

It flashes across the sky.

• What other lights do you see at night?

Dark places are where
light cannot reach.

It is dark inside a closet.
It is dark inside a **cave**.

It is dark at the bottom of the sea.
This diver uses a flashlight.

This fish
makes its
own light!

• Can you think of other dark places?

The balloons and bugle are **shiny**.
Their surface is very smooth.

The cookies and ball do not **shine**.
They are **dull**.

Firefighters

Light bounces off a **shiny** object.
It **reflects** the light.

Firefighters wear **shiny** strips.
These **reflect** light in dark places.

• Why should you wear reflective strips at night?

We use lights on
special days.

Candles light up
a birthday **party**.

People use candles when they pray.

22

Fireworks light up the night sky.
They make a lot of noise!

Lights and music
are good together.

IT'S MY BIRTHDAY!

*Read the story and look for words about **light**.*

I wake up.
I look out of my window.
The **sun** is **shining**.

What a great **day**
for my **party**!

The **light** outside
is very **bright**.
It hurts my eyes.

I put on my **dark** glasses.
Now I can **see**.

I go with Dad to
buy **party** food.

On the way, we see
flashing lights.

It's a **fire** engine!
"The **lights warn** us to
keep out of the way," says Dad.

When we get home, we get ready for the **party**.

The room is too **dark**. Dad opens the drapes.

Mom switches on the **lamp**. Now the room is much **brighter**!

Dad switches on the tiny **lights**. The little **bulbs** twinkle like **stars**.

We hang up my silver ball.

It is very **shiny**!

My friends arrive.

The **party** can begin!

We play lots of games.
We eat **party** food. Yummy!

It gets **dark** outside. It is **night**.

Mom switches off the
lights. The room is
dark like a **cave**.

We make scary
faces with a **flashlight**!

What is that **light**?
It is from the **candles**
on my birthday cake!

"The **flames** are hot,"
warns Dad.
I blow out the **candles**.

Now it is
time to watch
the **fireworks**.

I put on
a **shiny** belt.
It **reflects** the
light from cars.

It is a warm **night**.
The **stars** twinkle in the sky.
The **moon shines**.

Fireworks light up the sky. There is a big **bonfire**.

What a great birthday **party**!

Tell a story about a festival or **party** where there were **candles** or **lights**.

Draw a picture of **shining lights** or **fireworks**.

fireworks

QUIZ

Can you **see** in the **dark?**

Answer on page 5

Why should you be careful near a **fire?**

Answer on page 10

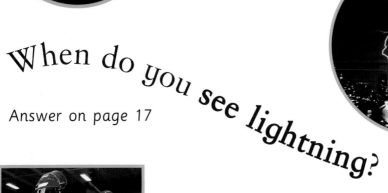

When do you **see lightning?**

Answer on page 17

How do **shiny** strips help in the **dark?**

Answer on page 21

Did you know the answers? Give yourself a

Do you remember these **light** words?
Well done! Can you remember any more?

 dark
page 5

sun
page 6

 bulb
page 8

candle
page 11

 flashing
page 13

bright
page 14

 moon
page 16

cave
page 18

 shiny
page 20

fireworks
page 22